The Ant and The Boy

This Book belongs to
....

For Patrick & Rowan

First published in the UK in 2022
by Book Bunny Publishing
info@bookbunnypublishing.com
www.bookbunnypublishing.com

Copyright © 2022 Patrick Mullins. All rights reserved.
Thank you for buying an authorised edition of this book and for complying with copyright laws. You are supporting writers and their hard work by doing this.

No part of this publication may be reproduced, stored in or introduced into a retrieval system, or transmitted, in any form, or by any means (electric, mechanical, photocopying, recording or otherwise) without the prior written permission of Patrick Mullins.

For information contact:
Patrick Mullins at www.TheAntAndTheBoy.com
or by email: patrick@theantandtheboy.com

Hardback ISNB 978 1 7391506 1 7
Paperback ISBN 978 1 7391506 0 0

Special thanks to Danielle Black for helping with spelling, grammar and editing.

www.TheAntAndTheBoy.com

TheAntAndTheBoy
TheAntAndTheBoy

The Ant and The Boy

Written & Designed By
Patrick Mullins

In a house just like this one, lived a little boy called Patrick, who dreamed of being a friendly giant. It was all he ever wanted.

One morning, Patrick went outside to play, where he saw a group of big children playing. He decided to go and join them.

He hopped, skipped and jumped over to them with a smile on his face.

But the big children didn't want to play with Patrick, they laughed at him, calling him a little boy,

"You're too little to play with us, you're a little boy," they said.

This made Patrick really sad.

"I am not a little boy, I'm a big boy," he told them.

But the big children didn't listen and continued to call him a little boy.

This made Patrick even more upset, and he walked away crying to himself.

As he walked away with a tear on his cheek, he spotted something on the ground...
A group of ants.
"I wonder if they will play with me?" He thought to himself.

So, he hopped, skipped and jumped over to them, with a smile back on his face.

The ants felt scared and worried, that Patrick might be an evil giant. So, they turned and quickly rushed back to their home.

Patrick got upset all over again, he sat down and started to sob. All he wanted to do was play with the ants.

As all the ants rushed back to their home, one brave ant looked back at Patrick and saw he was upset. He thought to himself,
"Maybe he's a friendly giant, not an evil one."

Because he was a brave ant, he turned and crawled back over to Patrick.

He crawled onto his foot,

Then up his leg,

Across his tummy,

Around his back,

Over his chest,

Around his neck and down his arm.

They laughed and played all day long.

At the end of the day, the brave ant had to go home.

He crawled up Patrick's arm,

Around his neck,

Down his chest,

Around his back,

Over his tummy,

Down his leg and over his foot. Making Patrick giggle and laugh again.

The brave ant waved goodbye to Patrick and then rushed home to the other ants.

The brave ant told the story of the wonderful day he'd had with the friendly giant called Patrick.

The very next day, Patrick went out to play. He was very excited to play with the brave ant again.

He hopped, skipped and jumped over to where the ants lived.

Patrick sat and waited for the brave ant to come out to play.

When he saw the brave ant appear, he was surprised to see he wasn't alone.

All the ants had come to play. This put a huge smile on his face.

Around his back,

Over his chest,

Around his neck and down his arms.

Patrick giggled and laughed for hours on end, as the ants crawled all over him.

The ant and the boy remain best of friends to this day.

Meet the real-life Boy from The Ant and The Boy

This is my little boy, who is also called Patrick. The Ant and The Boy was written for him while we were on holiday. He loves books and loves a good bedtime story. We had forgotten to pack any books, so one night, Patrick asked me to make up a bedtime story for him. Earlier that night, we had been on an ant hunt, and we were feeding the ants some sugar. So, I decided to make up a story about a boy and an ant, and this is how The Ant and The Boy was created.

Patrick loved the story so much, that he had me read it to him each night. He loved the part where the ants were crawling over the boy, I would tickle him as the ant crawled over him in the story, and this made him giggle and laugh. He asked me if I could make it into a real book, I promised him I would, and as you can see I kept that promise to my little boy.

We hope you have enjoyed reading, and your little ones had fun listening along. If you enjoyed the book, please leave us a review online. Thank you for reading The Ant and The Boy.

Big Patrick & Little Patrick

Please visit our website and follow us on social media.

www.TheAntAndTheBoy.com
f TheAntAndTheBoy
📷 TheAntAndTheBoy

Can you find the Brave Ant?

He's hiding amongst the other ants, let's see if you can spot him.

Can you answer some questions?

Why did the ants get scared and worried?

Why did the big children not want to play with Patrick?

What did Patrick dream of being?

www.ingramcontent.com/pod-product-compliance
Lightning Source LLC
Chambersburg PA
CBHW041705160426
43209CB00017B/1749